Taking and writing minutes

**Other titles from
Centre for Strategy and Communication**

How to become a brilliant presenter
Tess Woodcraft

Moving into management
Julia Braggins

Taking and writing minutes

Jan Burnell

Centre for Strategy and Communication

Centre for Strategy and Communication

Centre for Strategy and Communication is a centre for reflection and change.

We help individuals and organisations in the public and non profit sectors transform the way they communicate. Minutes are one of the ways an organisation speaks to itself – informs, involves, records and explains. Minutes are an important communication tool. The Centre's highly regarded training on taking and writing minutes is just one of a wide range of training courses we run for managers and administrators.

If you would like more information about the Centre's consultancy and training you can find our website on www.the-centre.co.uk
Or contact us on 020 7490 3030

First published 2004 by
Centre for Strategy and Communication
140 Old Street, London EC1V 9BW

© Centre for Strategy and Communication 2004

ISBN 0–9546315–2–8

Cartoons: Mike Turner

Produced for the Centre for Strategy and Communication by
Chase Publishing Services, Fortescue, Sidmouth, EX10 9QG
Printed in the European Union

Contents

Acknowledgements

This book distils my experience of both chairing and taking and writing minutes for all manner of meetings. But it owes a great debt to others, particularly my colleagues from the Centre for Strategy and Communication who have all given generously of their experience and skill in running and recording meetings. I could not have done it without them. Their knowledge, laughter and support has helped me to get all this down on paper.

The CSC is grateful to Elizabeth Mills, formerly of Research into Ageing, for permission to use the notes of a team meeting on page 37.

I also want to thank all the trainees whose experiences of minute taking – both good and bad – have truly enriched this book.

1
Introduction

Whether you are writing minutes for a small informal gathering or for a formal board, they will be considered as an important document. Once approved, the minutes are the one mutually agreed and official record of the meeting they describe. If 'it isn't in the minutes' then, in a very real sense, it didn't happen.

This is why so many people are nervous and unconfident about taking minutes. They know that, if things go wrong and the minutes are not felt to be correct, then this could have serious consequences for the group that held the meeting and for the individuals within that group.

This book has been written to help you write business-like, clear and concise minutes that deal accurately with the proceedings of the meeting and that leave out all the 'waffle'. It is based on years of experience both of minuting and of chairing meetings at a range of different levels and in all kinds of organisations including businesses, charities, local authorities and political parties.

The book deals with most aspects of minutes and attempts to give a clear answer, where there is one, to questions about good practice in minute taking. However, one of the fruits of experience is that all organisations are different, all meetings are different and the 'rules' do vary from organisation to organisation and from meeting to meeting. We attempt to deal with some of the variations here but would warn the minute taker that 'how we do things round here' is always worth bearing in mind.

If you want to become proficient at taking minutes, there is no substitute for practice. The best way is to shadow the official minute taker for a few sessions so that you can learn the rules and understand the meeting without the anxiety of being officially responsible for the minutes. If this is not possible then use one of the main lessons of this book – work with the chair of your meeting and enlist as much help as possible as you learn your trade.

We hope that you will find this book a useful starting point. Happy minuting!

"DO YOU HAVE A MINUTE?"

2
The purpose of minutes

A set of minutes can have many different purposes. Obviously, the main purpose is to act as the official record of the meeting but this can mean different things in different groups and organisations. Minutes can be extremely formal and have a legal status as in a local council meeting or they can be an informal set of notes that may be thrown away within a few weeks or days of the meeting.

When considering the purpose of the minutes you have to write, it is worth thinking about the nature of the meeting and the 'audience' the minutes will serve. Both of these factors, which we will go into in more detail below, will influence the purpose, and hence the style, of your minutes.

To be the official record of the meeting

The minutes constitute the agreed and official record of the meeting that they describe. For this reason, they should be both concise and clear (for ease of reading) and accurate and complete (so that everything important is recorded). Achieving the right balance between these two elements is one of the main difficulties for minute takers. Whatever the recollection of any of the individuals who attended the meeting, the minutes, once they have been agreed, are the **only** official record. If for example, Mr Green claims that the meeting agreed to pay travel expenses to all attenders but this was not recorded in the approved minutes, then no travel expenses can be paid (or not without a fresh, minuted decision).

To bind participants to mutually agreed decisions

Minutes should bind the participants to act in accordance with the decisions taken. If I do not feel that a particular decision was a good one, I must still act in accordance with it once it has been agreed in the minutes. I may even be bound to defend this decision, in line with my responsibilities to the group. Minutes therefore underline and underpin the collective nature of meetings and the decisions meetings take. Once taken, decisions are the property of the group and can only be changed by the group acting together. This principle of meetings is reinforced by recording decisions properly in a way that everyone can agree.

To record decisions made by the group

Decisions are one of the cornerstones of minutes. If the group is not making a decision, you may or may not need to record its proceedings. If it is making a decision, you **always** need to record it. Decisions are therefore one of your main 'filters' in deciding that crucial question for minute takers – what to put in and what to leave out (we will deal with the other filters later).

A very senior retired civil servant was asked by the local village hall committee to be their minutes secretary. At her first meeting, she sat quietly with her pad and pencil in front of her but wrote nothing for the first 20 minutes. The group were puzzled. 'Why aren't you writing anything down?' 'Because you haven't decided anything yet!' was the firm answer.

To record agreement or disagreement with decisions

This is a more difficult area. Some groups make all decisions by voting. Each question is 'put to the vote', hands raised and the number of votes for and against decided. In many ways, this is the easy option for the minute taker who will at least know exactly what the group has decided about each issue.

Most meetings do not have votes. Each item on the agenda is discussed until the chair or the group feel they have come to a conclusion and the group will then move on to the next item. A good chair will summarise what has happened so that the group are clear (see Chapter 5) but not all chairs do this. The minute taker has to pick up the sense of the discussion and summarise what they believe the group's consensus decision to have been. Being able to do this well is the secret of really excellent minute taking.

We will discuss later what to do if you don't know what the group has decided. The point here is that, in this kind of consensus-based group, it is not usually appropriate to record who agreed with the group's decision and who did not. Once the decision has been made, everyone is bound by it anyway so it may be unnecessary and even unhelpful to record who spoke on the different sides of the debate.

Indeed, our advice would be to keep names out of minutes altogether. The golden rule here is:

WRITE ABOUT WHAT THE MEETING DID, NOT WHAT THE PEOPLE SAID.

Example

Suppose Fred Green, Jill Verdi and Ajit Singh are discussing where to hold a conference and Fred and Jill favour Birmingham while Ajit thinks London is a better idea. Once the discussion is wound up, your minute will **not** read:

Fred spoke in favour of Birmingham because… And Jill supported him because… Ajit thought the conference should be held in London because…

It should read:

The group discussed whether the conference should be held in London or Birmingham. After discussion, the Birmingham venue was agreed.

However, there are some exceptions to this guideline:

- *When a speaker is giving an opinion or view as a specialist*

  This might be the treasurer talking about finance or the architect talking about buildings or the solicitor talking about a legal point. It clearly makes sense to record that the group was given specialist advice that either supported or opposed the decision it made. Where the group opposes the view of a specialist such as a treasurer or solicitor, you should try to record the group's reasons for this in the minutes

- *When the speaker asks for their disagreement with the decision to be recorded*

  If someone feels strongly enough to ask for their views to be recorded it is usually best to do so. Very rarely, where a decision could cause legal difficulties for the individuals within the group, such recorded disagreement could be important in protecting an individual from liability for a bad decision

- *When the group or the chair asks you to record individual views*

  This is an area where the 'how we do things round here' rule comes into play. Generally speaking, it is best practice to summarise in minutes, to be concise and to keep individuals' names and contributions to an absolute minimum. However, some individuals and groups like to see their names in print and will ask you to override this guideline. As the minute taker, you are the servant of the group: you should do what the group requires you to. However, be aware that in your next job, the best practice guideline will probably apply

To record who is responsible for carrying out the group's decisions – action points

In many sets of minutes, one of the most important purposes will be to set out who is responsible for implementing the decisions the group has made. This would apply to groups like team meetings, senior executive teams, project meetings and so on.

Where this is important, it is useful to lay out your minutes so that these 'action points' are clear and stand out from the page. We discuss this further in Chapter 6.

Not all meetings, however, will need action points. Where a meeting is primarily about governance issues, for example a trustee board in a large charity, it may be assumed that actions will be carried out by others (i.e. the staff of the charity). The rule of thumb is, therefore, to include action points where the meeting has a management focus and to exclude them where the meeting is primarily focused on governance with decisions being carried out by people other than the meeting participants.

As with many other aspects of these guidelines, the other rule of thumb is to follow usual practice in your own organisation: if your meetings usually have action points then include them – if they don't, don't.

To record the fact that information has been received by the meeting

As well as items concerned with decisions that the group must make, meetings also consider 'information items'. Sometimes these are specified as such on the agenda. They may relate to documents or information from outside the organisation such as a new government circular, or they may relate to internal information items such as management information about the organisation's work. Often such items will be minuted using the 'received and noted' format:

> *The group received the Government Circular on Red Tape and noted that it seemed very bureaucratic!*

To inform those not present at the meeting

One of the important purposes of minutes is to inform those who could not attend a particular meeting about what happened in their absence. They are still bound by the minutes even though they did not attend and should challenge any decisions they do not like under 'Matters arising from the Minutes' if necessary.

However, minutes are also used to inform wider groups about a particular meeting's proceedings, for reasons of transparency or in the interests of consultation. One example of this would be a staff working party on equal opportunities whose minutes might be copied to all staff so that they could comment on the group's work. Where minutes are used for wider circulation in this way, they must be written with this in mind. It may be necessary to go into a bit more detail, to use fewer acronyms and initials and to simplify the language, taking out any jargon, so that everyone who reads the minutes can understand them.

There is an important point about accessibility here. The minutes should be written so that each of their audiences can read them and understand them easily. Part of the purpose of minutes is to ensure accountability for the organisation or group's decisions. If the minutes cannot be understood, then they cannot be used to hold the group to account.

To act as a legal and historical record

Many minutes do not have legal or historical status or importance. The record of the admin team meeting may be a simple note that is kept as a record of agreed decisions and actions and discarded after a few weeks or months as no longer relevant.

However, any group with its own legal status such as a company, health trust, charity board, a school governing body, or a council committee will have minutes that have to be written, circulated and kept in ways specified in the governing document of the organisation. Such minutes form an important element of the history and archives of the organisation and are unlikely to be thrown away. They are also a vital part of the organisation's response to regulation. Good minutes demonstrate that the organisation is being run properly and that rules and laws are being kept. They are therefore an extremely important element of the organisation's administration and should be treated as such. Scrappy, incomplete, badly taken and badly filed minutes do nothing to enhance an organisation's effectiveness – or its reputation!

The importance of good minutes

An association decided to set up a charity to carry out particular activities that were outside its normal remit. Things went wrong and the Charity Commission were called in to sort them out. They took a poor view of the charity's administration and were minded to apply personal fines to the charity trustees. Amongst the reasons they gave for this were:

'Minutes of meetings were poor...'

Minutes are not...

- A verbatim record of discussions

  It is important not to attempt to record the contribution of each speaker in the minutes. Remember the golden rule set out above. It is the meeting's proceedings with which you are concerned and these are best recorded by a summary of the important points in the discussion rather than a blow-by-blow description of each point. We will discuss how to do this later on.

- **A rehearsal of all the arguments for and against decisions**

In the same way, it is unnecessary to record all the reasons why decisions were taken. Where the meeting reached a consensus easily and naturally, it may only be necessary to record the decision itself.

> *It was decided to hold the conference in Birmingham.*

Where a decision is more controversial, the **main** arguments on each side should be summarised.

> *Although a London venue was considered to have better facilities and refreshments, it was decided to hold the conference in Birmingham as that was where most of the participants would come from.*

- **About matters irrelevant to the meeting**

People often get carried away at meetings and can go off the subject, either talking about items that are not on the agenda or even about matters that are not relevant to this group at all! These should simply not be minuted.

3
Preparing for a meeting

As with most activities, taking minutes is much easier if you have undertaken a certain amount of preparation. Unfortunately, many managers have a false perception that anyone in an administrative role can easily take the minutes for any meeting, whether they are familiar with the subject matter or not. This is not the case! No one can take minutes for a meeting that they do not understand. Unlike the job of the court stenographer or a shorthand secretary, who is required simply to reproduce what is said, minute takers have to summarise and extract from the material they hear. This requires a degree of understanding and judgement that can only be acquired from a reasonable knowledge of the subjects under discussion.

The more familiar you are with the business of a particular meeting, the easier it will be to minute it. For this reason, it is a good idea to have a regular minute taker for each regular meeting and to encourage the minute taker to become familiar with the subject matter of the meeting. Being pulled in at the last minute to a meeting on a topic you know nothing about is enough to panic the most confident minute taker!

However, there are some simple actions you can take to make each meeting easier whether you are the regular minute taker or not.

Read the minutes of the last meeting

This is essential, whether you are a new minute taker or very familiar with the group. If the meeting is familiar, a quick review of the last set of minutes to remind yourself of the subject matter is probably all you need. If you are new to minuting this group, you will need to study the minutes, ask about or look up any unfamiliar terms, find out what the subject matter is likely to be and familiarise yourself with it if possible.

You will need to understand the terminology, any initials or acronyms used and any unfamiliar titles or phrases. For example, in the housing world, the term 'void' means an empty property for which no rent is being received. This is a very different use to the usual English term.

Read all the supporting papers

Some meetings have large packs of papers that accompany the agenda and form the subject matter for the meeting. Others have less accompanying paperwork. Either way you, as the minute taker, must be familiar with the main thrust of each accompanying paper.

For a busy administrator, this may seem like an unrealistic demand. You surely have better things to do with your life than read through reams of paperwork! However, there are various strategies for getting to understand a long document without reading all of it.

Read the executive summary

Nowadays, many longer documents have a summary either at the beginning or the end that gives the main points of the document. This is ideal for the minute taker as it will probably give you as much as you need to understand the discussion.

Look at the contents page or chapter and section headings

A glance at the contents page of the document will give you the flavour of its subject matter. It may be necessary to read a particular chapter or section in more detail if you think that this is likely to form the basis for your group's discussion.

Look at the conclusions or recommendations

Your group is likely to focus on these in discussion. Very often, the purpose of the discussion is to decide whether or not to agree the recommendations. You need to be familiar with these to understand the discussion.

What if the papers are tabled at the meeting?

It is very bad meeting practice to bring lengthy papers to the meeting which have not been previously circulated. Neither the chair nor any of the meeting participants will have had a chance to consider the papers, do any necessary research, consult colleagues or just form a view! If papers are tabled at the meeting, the chair should allow a few minutes for the group to read through them. As minute taker, this is your opportunity to draw attention to your need for careful summarising both during the discussion and at the point of any decision. However, the best option, if you can achieve it, is to outlaw tabled papers altogether.

Go through the agenda with the chair

A good chair will take the time to brief the minute taker on any aspect of the agenda that may be complex or where the minute taker might need support. A quick skim through the agenda before the meeting, ensuring that the minute taker understands the gist of each topic, will pay dividends both for the minute taker and for the chair.

Although many of those who chair meetings do not understand how useful this is, a good chair will always do this. Try to get the people who chair your meetings to give you a short time before the meeting – perhaps only five minutes – to complete this vital task. If necessary, you could show them this book! We will refer to this again in Chapter 5.

Ensure you understand enough to record decisions

All the strategies set out above are aimed at helping you to understand enough of the discussion to be able to record the decisions and action points. Other things you could do to help your understanding of your meetings are:

- Ask colleagues who regularly attend the meeting to brief you about unfamiliar topics
- Read professional journals to help your understanding of policies and practices

- Talk to your manager in supervision about any aspects of meetings you find particularly difficult to understand

Determine what kind of minutes or notes will be necessary

The easiest way to do this is to look at the last set of minutes. The structure, layout, numbering and style of the minutes is likely to be determined by following custom and practice for this meeting. If you are minuting the first meeting of a group, ask the chair to guide you as to how formal the minutes should be and how they would like them laid out.

Finally, a few very practical points…

Arrive at the meeting in plenty of time

As the minute taker, you must arrive at the meeting early. It may be your job to set the room up and arrange for refreshments. You will be expected to provide spare copies of any papers that were circulated and of the minutes of the last meeting, whether these were previously circulated or not.

It is also the case that your confidence will not be improved by arriving late, with your papers in a mess and having to look around for the last available seat in the room. Arrive early, have your papers in apple pie order, preferably in a ring-binder, with each agenda item clearly marked. This will mark you out as a professional minute taker, ensure respect from the group and improve your confidence at the start of the meeting.

Use this time at the beginning of the meeting to build your relationship with the chair. If the chair is your manager or another colleague, this may be unnecessary. However, many minute takers only meet the person who chairs the meeting at the meeting itself. If you can take a few minutes to greet them, offer them refreshments and generally make them feel welcome, this will help your relationship during the meeting. And, of course, you are going to encourage the chair to give you a short briefing on the agenda before the meeting starts!

Sit next to the chair

The minute taker and the chair should work in partnership to service the meeting. It is the chair's job to ensure that the meeting runs smoothly and the minute taker's job to record its decisions. Both of these roles depend on each other for their effectiveness. To this end, you should ideally be sitting at the top of the meeting table, next to the chair.

This will help you to work with the chair – to draw their attention to people trying to speak, to remind them to summarise decisions for the group and to call to their attention if the meeting is wandering off focus or getting out of hand. A good chair will understand and appreciate all these roles and will be keen to work with you. We will discuss this further in Chapter 5.

If the culture of your organisation or custom and practice do not allow the minute taker to sit next to the chair, try to sit in a position that allows you direct eye contact with the chair and a good sight line to each person attending the meeting. This will make it easier for you to work with the chair during the meeting and to understand the discussions.

Try to avoid being positioned at a separate table away from the meeting table. It will be far harder for you to hear and understand the discussion in this position and it is also disrespectful to the important role the minute taker is fulfilling.

Have a full set of papers, two pens and plenty of paper!

This may seem obvious but it can all too easily be forgotten. We have discussed the need to have your meeting papers well organised above. It is also important to have at least two pens, in case one goes wrong, and plenty of paper to write on. If your pens are of different colours, this will help you to mark up any gaps in your notes where you will need help after the meeting. Try to use a shorthand pad or a bound notebook to take notes at the meeting. This way, your notes will easily stay in the order in which you wrote them. If you use a pad where the pages are torn off as you write, you may get them out of order and this could prove difficult later! If you do use a tear-off pad, be sure to number several pages in advance.

Remember, preparation is a vital part of minute taking. A few minutes spent familiarising yourself and getting organised beforehand may save hours later.

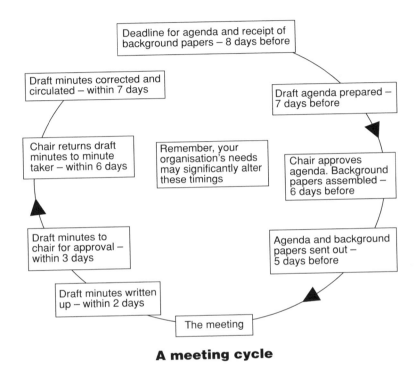

Deadline for agenda and receipt of background papers – 8 days before

Draft minutes corrected and circulated – within 7 days

Draft agenda prepared – 7 days before

Chair returns draft minutes to minute taker – within 6 days

Remember, your organisation's needs may significantly alter these timings

Chair approves agenda. Background papers assembled – 6 days before

Draft minutes to chair for approval – within 3 days

Agenda and background papers sent out – 5 days before

Draft minutes written up – within 2 days

The meeting

A meeting cycle

4
The role of the minute taker

The principal role of the minute taker is to ensure that the proceedings of the meeting are adequately recorded and that the record is properly circulated and archived. Within this overarching role, there are several elements.

Collate and circulate the agenda

The preparation of the agenda may be the responsibility of either the minute taker or the chair. Ideally, it will be done by the chair as they have to control and guide the meeting. For this reason, we have given guidelines about how to prepare the agenda in Chapter 5. However, the circulation of the agenda and the background papers is usually the responsibility of the minute taker. You should ensure that the chair is happy with the agenda before it goes out and that all the background papers have been received (see Chapter 3).

Background papers should be clearly marked with their agenda item number or a letter which refers to the agenda. For example:

4   *Building closure   Paper A*

This way, participants can be sure they are looking at the correct paper and can see how the papers relate to the agenda items.

Where there are a lot of background papers, it is sometimes a good idea to colour code them. One way is to photocopy each paper on a different colour paper, to help participants steer their way through the pile of papers. Another way is to code various functions of the organisation with different colours. One organisation used white for previous minutes, blue for finance, green for field work, pink for membership and so on.

With the chair you need to identify whether any participants need papers translated, on tape or in braille or large print.

Take notes that you can understand

In order to record the meeting properly, the minute taker takes notes during the meeting. We go into detail about how to take notes in Chapter 13. However, it is important to be clear at this point that the minute taker's notes are not the official record of the meeting but are an *aide memoire* for the minute taker's personal use. They do not need to be kept after the full minutes have been written and it is inappropriate for the meeting to ask to refer to them if there is disagreement about what happened at a previous meeting.

Unlike a journalist's notes from an interview, the minute taker's notes are entirely unofficial and have no status apart from their use by the minute taker. For this reason, your notes can be as scrappy and incomplete as you like as long as they record the points you need to write the minutes up afterwards. No one should need to see your notes apart from you!

Record those present and any apologies

It is very important to get the names of every meeting participant correct in the minutes. Incorrect spelling of names is bad manners and inconsistent with anti-discriminatory practice. Never assume you know how to spell a name – even names such as Ann/Anne or Sara/Sarah can lead you into difficulties.

If you do not know all the meeting participants, the easiest way to prevent problems in this area is to circulate an attendance list at the beginning of the meeting. If you wait until everyone has sat down and circulate the list round the table from one end, you will have a useful 'map' of the meeting table as well as a correct record of all the names of participants. As long as you know who one or two people are, you can now work out the names of all the other participants from their position on your attendance list.

Your attendance list should be a prepared table, rather than a piece of blank A4. There should be at least two columns – 'Print' and 'Sign'. This will ensure that they print their name properly at least once! You may also want to include columns for telephone number, email address and so on. If you do this, leave enough room for people to write their details – nothing is more irritating than trying to complete a form when the boxes are too small for the information!

It is often helpful, if participants do not know each other well, to prepare pieces of card, folded once, in front of each place with plenty of magic marker pens on the table. Participants can be asked to write their name on these, which makes the meeting easier for everyone. If you use prepared cards, don't put them out on the meeting table but ask people to collect them as they sit down. Remember there are always participants who put their name card down facing the wrong way round, so you might consider writing the name on both sides!

Ensure that all decisions are recorded

Your main function, as we have said, is to record the meeting's decisions. You must keep listening for these and for any and all points that relate to a particular decision and the reasons for making it.

Record the main reasons for decisions

Particularly where a decision is unusual, controversial or sensitive you will record the main reasons why it was made. You may also record some of the principal arguments made against the decision or in favour of other possible options. There is a careful balance here between verbatim recording of discussions and a concise summary of the main points made for and against during the discussion (we cover this in more detail in Chapter 9).

Record any information received

The meeting may 'receive' papers it does not choose to discuss. For example, a government consultation document may be felt to be too lengthy for the meeting to consider. It is important to record, in these cases, that the meeting has received the information and noted it.

The meeting received a consultation paper from the local Primary Care Trust on Working with Substance Misuse. The paper was noted.

Work with the chair to ensure decisions are clear

Throughout the meeting, the minute taker should work with the chair of the meeting to ensure that decisions are clearly made and can be clearly recorded. Where a vote is taken, the minute taker should be clear what was put to the vote, e.g. the exact wording of any motion or resolution, how many votes were recorded for and against and how many people abstained (see Chapter 11).

However, the much more usual situation is for the meeting to arrive at a decision through consensus. When this happens, it is the chair's duty to sum up the decisions the meeting has taken. If the chair does not do this, it is the minute taker's duty to politely prompt them – 'Excuse me, Chair, could you just summarise the decision on that item for the minutes.' Never feel out of place or stupid in asking for this – if you haven't understood the decision, it is likely that others at the meeting have not understood it either.

In very formal meetings, or where you do not work with the chair regularly, it may not be considered appropriate for you, as the minute taker, to interrupt the meeting. In these circumstances, make a big star in your notes and remember to ask the chair to give you guidance immediately after the meeting. It is much better to ask the chair (or another colleague if that is easier or more appropriate) than to make something up that may be inaccurate. All good chairs will support this kind of intervention from the minute taker and will understand your role as you understand theirs.

What if the chair (or the meeting) ask you to leave something out or minute something 'wrong'?

It sometimes happens that the chair, or a meeting participant, will ask you to leave something out of the minutes. This often happens where the discussion relates to an individual whose interests might be damaged if the discussion became general knowledge.

In these circumstances your guiding rule, as always, is to do what you are advised by the chair. It may be entirely appropriate that a personal remark which is not significant to the discussion is omitted from the minutes. In the same way, a sensitive discussion may be omitted in order to protect the organisation from difficulties. These kinds of decisions are for the meeting and the chair to make. The minute taker's role is to record what they are asked.

Sometimes the minute taker and the chair (or someone else) have a difference of opinion about what happened at the meeting and, in particular, what the decision on an item was. Again, the chair has the guiding role here and their decision will be the important one. When the minutes are put to the next meeting, the meeting itself will decide if anything important has been omitted or changed. Once the minutes have been approved by the meeting, that is the official record and that, in an important sense, is what 'really' happened.

If you feel strongly that a meeting is suppressing vital information in a way which is either illegal or improper, your best course of action is to advise your line manager or another appropriate colleague of this. They can then help you decide what action should be taken. However, these very grave situations are quite rare and the rest of the time, the chair's word will be the final one.

"*LEAVE OUT THAT DECISION TO GIVE THE MINUTE TAKER A LARGE BONUS.*"

What if I get sent out of the meeting?

It is the unfortunate practice of some meetings to ask the minute taker to leave the room, either to stock up the refreshments or to undertake extra photocopying. If possible, this should be resisted by making alternative arrangements for this kind of help and reminding the chair about these before the meeting.

If you are sent out of the room, hand the chair your pad and ask them to minute the meeting while you are absent. This will ensure that at least the chair cannot blame you for any lapses in the minutes at that point. It may also prevent your being asked to leave again!

Produce an accurate and timely record of meetings

You must write your minutes up as soon as you can. The best time to write them up is on the same day as the meeting. If this is not possible, you should try to write them, if at all possible, within 48 hours of the meeting. Your memory can only hold so much information and the more time that has elapsed since the meeting, the less you will remember about what happened. Your notes are likely to take you only so far, so writing up the minutes quickly makes sense as well as getting a difficult job out of the way!

Managers and colleagues are often less than understanding about the need to do this. You can calculate that you will need approximately the same amount of time to write up your minutes as the meeting itself lasted. A one hour meeting takes about one hour to write up and so on. Diary management and assertive negotiation with managers and colleagues are important in ensuring that you have the necessary amount of time available as soon as possible after the meeting finishes. The more meetings you minute, the more important this is. A backlog of several sets of minutes, all of them for meetings that took place weeks ago, is both inefficient and depressing.

Your draft minutes will be checked by the chair of the meeting and we discuss this further in the next chapter. After this, there are different practices. Some groups want the draft minutes sent out immediately so that participants can take note of the action points and get on with them. This is particularly important for management focused meetings such as team meetings. Other groups prefer the minutes to go out with the agenda for the next meeting. This is more common for boards and other governance focused meetings. You will need to find out what your group requires.

Where the minutes are not circulated immediately, it is sometimes advisable to circulate a brief action sheet, showing the main action points agreed. Local authorities often do this for council and committee meetings. An action sheet is produced and circulated within, say, 48 hours of the meeting while the minutes themselves may be circulated later. It is important to head the action sheet carefully so that it cannot be confused with the official minutes.

Circulate the minutes to the relevant people

The minute taker should have an accurate circulation list for each meeting they minute. This should be kept up to date and should include the status of everyone circulated, for example member, observer, in attendance, ex officio and so on.

This is particularly important where meetings have two parts, one open and one confidential. In these circumstances, it is a good idea to print the confidential minutes (and agenda) on a different colour paper. This ensures that it is not confused with the open minute and is circulated to the correct people, stored in a locked cabinet and so on.

The list should also include details of participants' needs for translated minutes, taped version, braille or large print.

The status of the minute taker

It is unfortunately the case that minute takers can have very low status at some meetings. If you are minuting your own team meeting, this is unlikely to be a problem. However, if you are called in to minute a board meeting where you may not know the participants or be known to them, it is sometimes difficult to maintain your credibility. Many minute takers feel very nervous when minuting meetings full of strangers on subjects which are unfamiliar to them. We have given you lots of tips to overcome this throughout this book but another aspect to consider is the way you come over to the meeting participants.

If you are nervous, it is worth taking the trouble to dress in clothes which make you feel comfortable but which also project a professional and smart image. A suit, with a tie for men, will undoubtedly help you come over as a serious and professional person. If you couple this with a confident and assured manner (no matter how you feel inside!) you will find that the meeting takes you more seriously and that this makes it easier for you to carry out your role effectively.

The minute taker as a participant

It is quite common in team meetings for the minute taker to be a team member, often taking their turn on the 'minutes rota'. Trying to have your say in discussion while taking notes and remaining impartial is very difficult.

One way to avoid these difficulties, especially if you are not asked to minute often, is to ask a colleague to raise any points you would have made on your behalf. This means you will only have to speak on unexpected items and should keep your contribution down to the bare minimum.

If you do get caught up in discussion, stop the group, with the help of the chair, and ask for guidance:

> 'OK, colleagues, how would you like me to minute that last discussion?'

The minute taker as chair

Even more difficult than trying to minute while participating, is trying to minute while chairing. This should be avoided where possible.

If you have to take minutes of a meeting where you are the chair, then stop the meeting at the end of each agenda item, review your notes quickly and take a moment or two to jot down any points you may have missed. If necessary, use your chair's summarising role to check with the meeting that you have understood the decision. As the chair, there is no excuse for getting the decision wrong! The meeting should be happy to allow you time to do this. If they are not, suggest someone else takes the minutes!

5
The role of the chair

The chair's role is vital in ensuring an effective meeting and a good chair can be a minute taker's best ally. Unfortunately, a bad chair can make a minute taker's job very difficult. Below we look at the role of the chair and examine some ways in which minute takers can encourage good practice in the people who chair their meetings.

The chair's role: before the meeting

Decide on the purpose and objectives of the meeting

The chair should have a clear idea, before the meeting starts, as to the nature and purpose of the meeting and of each agenda item. 'It's Tuesday and we always meet on Tuesdays' is not good enough!

Clearly this is not possible if an agenda has not been prepared beforehand. Even an informal team meeting should make the effort to prepare an agenda in advance, perhaps by asking people to email the chair or the minute taker with points they want to raise. If this is not done, it is difficult to see how you could tell whether or not the meeting was necessary.

One example of the chair's role in preparation might be an agenda item headed 'Budget Report'. This could be a report back on performance against an existing budget or it could be a consultation item so that the group could make decisions about future budgets or it could be an information item on decisions made elsewhere about the team's budget. The chair needs to be clear about these kinds of differences so that they can steer the meeting through the appropriate kind of discussion. When they do this, the minute taker has a clearer idea of the kinds of decision the group is being required to make and it is easier to record the decisions.

Reflect on other participants' objectives

The chair needs to have an understanding of the perspectives and 'agendas' of all the participants at the meeting. For example, in a discussion about next year's budget, the finance officer might want to keep staff salaries low in order to stay within financial limits whereas the personnel officer might want salaries to rise in line with staff expectations. If the chair is aware of these kinds of differences, they can moderate the discussion so that everyone has a say and all points of view get heard. When this is done, the minute taker has a clearer idea of the discussion points and how they relate to the decision taken.

Draw up the agenda, grouping connected items together

Once the items for the agenda have been received, the chair will decide how to group them in a logical order. In some organisations, this job may fall to the minute taker. If this is the case, do try to get the chair to review and approve the agenda before it is circulated. They are going to have to run the meeting and it makes sense for them to have a clear understanding of the agenda beforehand.

Some meetings group agenda items by subject, for example all the finance items together, then all the staffing items. Others group the decision items first and then the less important information items. It is the job of the chair to decide this in accordance with the needs of the meeting.

Draw up a rough timing for the meeting – overall and for each agenda item

The chair should have a clear idea, before the meeting begins, of how long the meeting will take and how long to allow for each agenda item. Once decided, the timings should be printed on the agenda.

Example

10.00   *1*   *Welcome and apologies*

10.05   *2*   *Minutes of the previous meeting held on 20 June 2002*

10.10   *3*   *Matters Arising*

This should not be seen as a rigid straightjacket. However, if the printed agenda indicates timings for each item, it makes it much easier for the chair to ensure that all the business is reached within a reasonable time. If this is impossible, then agenda planning and the length, and perhaps the frequency, of the meeting may need to be reviewed.

Go through the agenda with the minute taker

As discussed in Chapter 3, the chair should take time to brief the minute taker on the agenda. Many minute takers (and some chairs) think of this as an unimaginable luxury. However, in a local authority setting for example, the chair of a council committee would not dream of chairing a meeting without a full briefing from the officers. This kind of preparation is just as important for minute takers who need, as we have pointed out, a good understanding of the meeting context in order to record its proceedings.

The chair and the minute taker are going to work together during the meeting. The few minutes briefing at the start is a way of making this partnership begin to work and helping each to appreciate the other's important role.

Where the meeting is either lengthy or particularly important (such as for an Annual General Meeting), a 'Chair's Briefing' is sometimes prepared. This is like a very detailed version of the agenda which spells out exactly what is required at each stage of the meeting. If this is done, the minute taker should have a copy.

Example

Section of Chair's Briefing

...

Nominations for Executive

Three nominations have been received so far. There are five places to fill. Nominations can be taken from the floor of the meeting. You should get a mover and a seconder and the names should be written down and handed to the chair/minute taker. Put each nomination to the vote and count votes for, against and abstentions. John Smith and Abdul Mohamed will act as tellers. Go on to the next item when the vote has been put and announce the vote to the meeting when the tellers have finished counting.

...

The chair's role: during the meeting

Open the meeting, welcome participants and, where appropriate, do introductions

The chair should declare the meeting formally open and get everyone to settle down before formally starting the meeting. If some or all of the participants are not known to the group, the chair should encourage introductions, either by welcoming people personally or by asking them to introduce themselves. As minute taker, it is a good idea to look carefully at each person you do not know and say their name, in your head, as loud as you can. This kind of mental repetition will help you remember who they are later on.

Announce each item and give a brief summary of what the meeting needs to do about it

It is up to the chair to make sure that the meeting knows the purpose of each agenda item, as discussed above. This should be shared with the meeting at the beginning of the item so that the discussion is kicked off to a good start.

For example, the chair might say:

> 'The next item is the Budget Report. We're being asked to consider and approve the draft budget submitted by the finance department. On page four of the report there are three options and we need to choose one.'

When the chair summarises the subject matter and purpose of the agenda item in this way, the minute taker knows exactly what to listen for and note down in order to record the significant items of discussion.

Ensure that discussion stays focused and keeps roughly to time

It is the chair's job to ensure that discussion stays focused and does not stray away from the item on the agenda. Where participants are keen to discuss another related topic it is sometimes a good idea to 'park' this – i.e. agree to discuss it but at another time, perhaps under Any Other Business. The chair should also prompt the meeting to move on where necessary, ensuring that business is dealt with promptly without dominating the meeting inappropriately or rushing discussion. A timed agenda will help this process enormously (see above).

Ensure that all participants have a say

The chair should ensure that everyone who wants to can contribute to the discussion. This means keeping a reasonable level of control so that the meeting is not dominated by two or three strong people and so that quieter people can make their voices heard. The minute taker can help by quietly drawing the chair's attention to a person who seems to want to speak but can't get in to the discussion.

It is also the chair's role to ensure that everyone is able to contribute which may mean working with sign interpreters, community language interpreters, or setting out the room to support those needing to lip read.

Damp down participants who are dominating the discussion

This is part of the same requirement that the meeting conduct its business in a fair and respectful way so that everyone's voice is heard and no one can overwhelm the meeting with their own point of view. When the chair does this well, the minute taker finds it much easier to follow the discussion and to record it.

Sum up the decisions made at the end of each item

At the end of the discussion, the chair must tell the meeting what has been decided. This is particularly important in consensus style meetings where no vote is taken but agreement is assumed at the end of the discussion. It is in these circumstances that minute takers have great difficulty as they often have no idea what decision, if any, has been taken. Unfortunately, neither does anyone else!

It is essential that the chair summarises what they believe the decision to be so that the meeting can agree this and move on. When this is done, the minute taker can be certain what decision to record and has a much better notion as to what were the significant and relevant points during the discussion. If necessary, the minute taker must be prepared to prompt the chair to summarise in this way (see Chapter 4).

Ensure that the minute taker has noted all relevant points

After summarising and before moving on to the next item, a good chair will quietly check with the minute taker that they have all the information they need for the minute. This need be no more than a very quick visual check to see if the minute taker is looking relaxed and confident. If you need help at this point, a panic-stricken or rueful facial expression will usually do the trick and prompt a further summary. Some chairs will expressly ask the minute taker 'Are you all right on this for the minutes?' but most of the time this should not be necessary.

The chair's role: after the meeting

Allow a realistic but short deadline for the production of the draft minutes

The chair should be mindful of the time constraints on the minute taker. On the other hand, they should be aware of the need to produce minutes quickly. Since the chair must check draft minutes, they too will need a good memory of the meeting and they are unlikely to have taken such copious notes! It may be important for there to be some negotiation between the minute taker's line manager and the chair to ensure that expectations on both sides are clear and understood.

Read the minutes in draft and correct them

It is the responsibility of the chair to ensure that the minutes are as near correct as possible before they are presented to the next meeting. Where the minute taker is the formal secretary of the group or where both the chair and the minute taker are team members taking their turn on a rota, this is less important. In most situations, the minute taker is not a member of the group. The chair must therefore be responsible for the minutes on behalf of the group and present them to the group at the next meeting.

Minute takers often feel that chairs are unnecessarily 'picky' with the minutes. It is certainly the case that some managers cannot resist the temptation to mark up any document on which they are asked to comment. However, your chair, as a member of the group, has the right to frame the minutes as they feel appropriate. If they want more detail, try to give them this. If they consistently cross out a lot of what you have written, try to summarise more.

It is also the case that the chair will have a clearer understanding of the need for sensitivity than you might have. In one organisation, the minute taker accurately recorded:

> *The board noted that the organisation was no longer trading while insolvent.*

'Trading while insolvent' is unlawful and organisations that do this can be penalised heavily. The chair rewrote the minute:

> *The board noted the improved financial position of the organisation.*

While the original phrase was undoubtedly an accurate record, the revised version was the correct one in the circumstances.

Note that the minutes are still 'draft' after the chair has checked them. Only the meeting can approve or agree the minutes. However, once the chair has approved the minutes, they should not be altered again, except at the meeting. This will ensure that, at the meeting, everyone is correcting the same copy!

Return them to the minute taker promptly

Do not allow the chair to sit on the minutes for a long time. Even if you do not need to circulate the draft minutes quickly, it is bad practice for the minutes not to be signed off quickly and may lead to papers getting lost. It is best to give the chair a reasonable deadline – a few days at most – and politely but firmly indicate that you will expect this to be adhered to.

Take responsibility for the minutes at the next meeting

Having checked the minutes, the chair is now responsible for them as we have discussed above. If the meeting decides the minutes are incorrect, this is as much the responsibility of the chair as it is of the minute taker since they have checked them and taken responsibility for them – not all chairs realise this!

Take responsibility for chasing up action

It sometimes happens that the minute taker is expected, since they wrote the action points, to follow them up and ensure they happen. This is not necessarily part of the minute taker's role. It is for the chair to ensure that actions agreed by the meeting are carried out. This task is sometimes delegated to the minute taker but this remains a delegated responsibility and should not be assumed to form part of the minute taker's duties.

6
Formal or informal?

One question that often concerns minute takers is whether to record formal minutes or more informal notes. As with many matters relating to minutes, the best way of deciding is to ask your chair and do what they tell you. However, in the absence of such advice, here are some guidelines.

When to use informal notes

Informal meetings

By this we mean meetings that do not form part of the formal decision making structure of the organisation and that do not have their own standing orders, rules, terms of reference or constitution. Any meeting important enough to have a set of rules about how it should be run, whether these are called standing orders, a constitution, terms of reference or whatever, is important enough to have a formal minute taken of its proceedings.

The gathering of a few colleagues to plan a big night out to celebrate a festival will almost certainly warrant only an informal note of its decisions. Board meetings always have formal minutes. Between these extremes are a wide variety of shades of grey where you will have to make a judgement as to the level of formality required.

One-off meetings

If a meeting is a one-off, it is less likely to need formal minutes (though this is not a complete certainty). Meetings that are regular and form part of a coherent chain of events, such as a management team meeting, are more likely to have formal minutes.

When only the participants will be copied in

If only the meeting participants will read the minutes, it is fine to make them informal and relatively scrappy. However, even if the meeting was informal and relatively unimportant, if the record is going to be circulated to a wider group of people it is probably safer to record more formal minutes. In these circumstances, the reputation of the organisation may be involved and a set of scrappy informal notes may give the wrong impression.

When notes are not intended for formal storage

The most important guideline for formal or informal minutes is the length of time they will be kept and stored. Informal notes are thrown away as soon as they have been used. Formal minutes are filed and archived and kept forever. Again, between these extremes are a wide variety of practices but, in the main, if your minutes will be filed you should probably keep them formal.

Differences between notes and minutes

Notes do not need to use complete sentences

One of the main differences between a set of formal minutes and an informal note is that the latter need not use whole sentences. *'Jane to book the restaurant and order food.'* This is fine for an informal note. In a formal minute, this would read *'It was agreed that Jane Smith would book the restaurant and order the food.'*

Brevity must be combined with clarity. Don't abbreviate your sentences so much that other people can't understand them. *'Jane – restaurant and food'* is probably not enough.

First names are probably acceptable in informal notes

In a small informal group such as a team meeting, the use of first names only in minutes is acceptable. However, in the list of those present, do at least use an initial to distinguish exactly who was present at the meeting. There are often several people in an organisation with the same first name and confusion can arise. Never use first names on their own in formal minutes. Either the person's whole name should be used – Asif Singh – or their job title or role – the Information Officer or the Chair.

Abbreviations and acronyms can be used in informal notes

These are fine in informal notes – everyone who will read the notes understands them and knows the context in that they were used. However, in a formal minute, these are less acceptable. At the very least, it is good practice to use the whole phrase in the first instance and put the initials in brackets. These can then be used on their own later. For example: *'The National Society for the Prevention of Cruelty to Children (NSPCC)…'*

Action points pulled out as a separate column

An informal note is very likely to include action points and these should be clearly highlighted. Formal minutes may also include such action points although they may not: see Chapter 2 on the purpose of minutes for when to use action points. When action points are used, they can be highlighted using a column on the right hand side of the page with the initials of the person responsible opposite the action point in the minutes. A deadline for the action point should also be shown.

Example

	Action
The information officer will be responsible for	*Colin Smith*
bringing the leaflets to the meeting.	*By 8 March*

Another way of drawing attention to the action point is to align it on the right hand side of the page using bold type, for example:

Action: JB by 7 Sept

A helpful minute taker will take the trouble to mark each person's action points on their own copy of the minutes, perhaps using highlighter pen. This way, the recipient can see at a glance what they have to do as a result of the meeting.

Here is an example of the same discussion, first recorded as an informal note and then as a formal minute.

Example – Informal note

Notes of the Conference Sub Group held on 31   ACTION

December 2002

Present: Jan B, Fred S, Sharma K, Paul J

Apologies: Lucy

2.   **Notes of the last meeting**

Agreed.

3.   **Annual conference 2003**

Jan reported that all the main speakers were booked.

These were Bill Bryan, Jenny Wren and Nora Parker.

The CE would also give a presentation on the organisation's work.

JAN

Paul gave a list of workshop titles that his team had produced. These were:

- Listening to our customers
- Equal opportunities
- Newsletters and leaflets

The group decided to add the following:

- Presentation skills for volunteers
- Fundraising for local groups   PAUL

We need two more workshops – please would everyone think of at least one title, preferably with a speaker, and let Jan know ASAP.

ALL

Example – Formal minute

Minutes of a meeting of the Conference Sub Group held on 13 November 1997 at the office of the organisation

Present: Jan Burnell, Director of Information Services

Fred Smith, Information Manager South

Paul Johnson, Information Manager North

Sharma Kaur, Publications Officer

CSG/31/97   Apologies

These were received from Lucy McDonnell, Finance Officer

CSG 32/97   Minutes of the last meeting

These were agreed as a correct record

CSG/33/97   Matters arising

There were no matters arising

CSG/34/97   Annual Conference 1997

(1)   *Workshops*

The Director of Information Services reported that the main speakers had been booked. These were: Bill Bryan, Minister, Jenny Wren, chief executive of Care Org, and Nora Parker, agony aunt and columnist. The Chief Executive would also give a presentation on the work of the organisation.

The Information Manager North reported on workshop titles suggested by his team. These were: Listening to our customers, Equal Opportunities and Producing a Newsletter. After discussion, it was agreed that the following titles would be added: Presentation Skills for Volunteers and Fundraising for Local Groups.

It was agreed that further workshops were needed and Sub Group members were asked to contact the Director of Information Services with suggestions for titles and speakers as soon as possible.

Case study

Notes of a team meeting

Notes of staff meeting held on Monday, 13 December, 1999

Present: Jo (Chair), Simona, Laura M, Nisha, Laura S, Lisa, Andrew, Andrea, James, Katie, Martin

Apologies: Sarah, Caroline and Elizabeth

1. **Matters arising**   Action

   Telephones
   We have received a quote from Samsung for the installa-
   tion of an additional 2 phones (and connections), one for Jo   Jo
   and the other for the post desk. It is hoped we can arrange
   for this to take place shortly.

   New volunteer
   The new volunteer that Sarah hoped would come into the
   office and provide some admin support has decided against
   joining us. On trying out the journey, she found it too far to
   manage on a regular basis.

   Staff
   It was agreed that to save confusion, all staff will be referred
   to by their first names as opposed to using their initials.

Kitchen and Post Duties
Everyone was reminded that when on kitchen duty, they now
need to help Andrea, on one day, with post opening when
Laura S is not in. Jo was reminded that Laura M and Martin   All
should not be put on kitchen duty together as neither are
allowed to open post.

2. **Staff holidays**

   No additional holidays were given. Simona told staff how
   many days they had available to take and that only 5 days
   leave could be carried forward to next year. The remainder
   will be lost.

3. **Coffee**

   It was agreed that the charity would only supply Nescafé (or
   equivalent). Any staff member wishing to use Fair Trade
   coffee/tea, or any other type of coffee, should do so at their
   own cost (as is the current practice regarding fruit teas).

4. **Deliveries**

   All staff were asked, as far as possible, to check the items
   they were signing for and if possible, to get the recipient to
   sign for it.

   Cold callers
   Various problems have arisen recently with companies cold
   calling and offering discounts on goods we use (that actually
   turn out to cost more!). It was asked that all staff say
   something along the lines of: they do not have the authority
   to order goods; it's not the charity's policy to place orders
   over the phone; that we are happy with our current suppliers.

   Persistent callers can be told politely to go away – and then
   hung up on!

5. **Minutes**

   The question was raised over whether the person chairing
   the staff meeting should also take minutes. It was agreed
   that as this was only likely to happen once every 14 weeks,
   it wasn't a problem. It was further agreed that anyone who
   wished to call upon a staff member to help them out, is free
   to do so.

6. **Any other business**

   Laura S
   Simona reported that Laura S will be working 3 days a week. Laura will be in the office every Monday to take part in the weekly meetings. The remaining days will be decided the preceding week and staff will be informed as soon as possible so that people on kitchen duty are aware of their post duty days.

   Staff Christmas party
   Jo will circulate menus for various restaurants. It was asked that all staff indicate their preference and return the list to Jo as soon as possible so that a venue could be booked.   Simona

   Fundraising software
   Andrew reported that the cut off date for the old software would be sometime between Wednesday and Friday. Please note: The last date for inputting/changing details is Thursday evening.   All

7. Chair of Next Meeting: Lisa

7
The structure of minutes

Layout and structure

There are many ways of setting out minutes and different organisations have different rules for this. It is helpful to minute takers, and looks more business like, if there is a 'house style' for each organisation so that all the minutes have the same structure and layout. In this chapter, we give you some rules and some guidelines to help you decide how to structure and lay out your minutes. We have also included an example of one organisation's house style.

Heading

The title of the minutes should include the name of the group, the time and date of the meeting and the venue where it took place. In formal minutes, in particular, the venue is important. This establishes that these are the minutes of the official meeting for which the calling notice went out – not the unofficial meeting that took place at the pub over the road!

Example

Minutes of a meeting of the Regeneration Partnership Steering Group held at 7.30 pm on 20 September 2002 at County Hall

List those present

Most minutes will include two lists at the beginning. The first includes those who are 'Present' and includes members of the meeting who are entitled to take part in decision-making and, where necessary, vote on decisions. The second list is often described as 'In Attendance' and lists anyone who attended the meeting but was not a member of it. A charity trustee board meeting would only record the trustees as present. Any other staff at the meeting such as the chief executive, would be recorded as in attendance. In the same way, a local council would record only the councillors as present while the staff attending the meeting would be recorded as in attendance.

It is important to distinguish between these two lists because it is only the members of the meeting who can form the quorum. The quorum is the minimum number of people who must be present at the meeting for it to have official status and take binding decisions. The number for the quorum will be established in the terms of reference, constitution or Memorandum and Articles for the group. If no such document exists for the meeting – for example in the case of a team meeting – then distinguishing between those present and those in attendance is less important (although it is still best practice to do so).

When recording those present, you should list their full name, with title where appropriate, their role at the meeting, if any, and the group or organisation they represent if they are attending as a representative. Thus, at an interagency meeting, the local authority representative who is also the chair of the meeting would be listed as follows:

Raoul Finestre, Local Authority (Chair)

It is often best to list people in alphabetical order of their last name. This is a simple system to follow and easy to justify. Some groups list the chair of the meeting first. However, we would advise against trying to list people in order of their importance to the meeting. This could get you into a lot of trouble!

Where someone is not present for the whole of the meeting (and the meeting has a quorum), you should indicate this in the list, for example:

Sylvia Andreou, Police Authority (part only)

You should then record in the text of the meeting the point at which they joined or left the meeting:

Sylvia Andreou left the meeting at this point.

Some organisations indicate the point at which people joined or left the meeting in the list of those present. This is perfectly acceptable.

However, do not indicate their arrival or departure by the time of day. The group needs to know which part of the meeting they attended and this will not be made clear by using the time of day.

So, do put:

Sylvia Andreou, Police Authority (arrived after Item 4)

Don't put:

Sylvia Andreou, Police Authority (arrived at 11.30 a.m.)

By and large, this convention is only important for the kind of formal meeting which has a constitution or terms of reference. For less formal meetings such as team meetings, it is probably unnecessary to do this. As always in minuting, when in doubt, ask the chair.

Apologies

This is likely to be the first item on the agenda. Do not record the apologies of people who are not present but have not sent their apologies to the meeting. The purpose of this item is to allow members of the meeting to 'receive' the apologies of those who have given them. It is at least hypothetically possible for the meeting to refuse to accept a member's apologies, for example if they have not attended for a long time. Many organisations have rules that state that if a member does not attend and does not send apologies for a certain number of meetings – often three meetings – then they may be deemed to have resigned from the group. Clearly, in these cases, it would be unhelpful to record apologies if people have not given them.

Members of staff who are on sick leave or annual leave are deemed to have given their apologies for all the meetings they would have attended had they been at work.

Some chairs and some meetings like a list of those who were absent included in the minutes. If you are asked to include this, make it quite separate from the apologies, perhaps with a heading – 'Absent'. Be guided by the chair on this point.

If someone has given their apologies, you should check the previous minutes and see if they had any action points. If they did, try to find out what progress has been made so that you can report to the meeting.

Minutes of the last meeting

The next agenda item allows the group to approve or agree the minutes of the previous meeting as a correct record. Discussion on this item should only relate to whether or not the minutes are accurate. Discussion on the content of the minutes should take place under 'Matters Arising' (see below). In the heading for this minute, you should always record the date when the last meeting took place. For example:

Minutes of the previous meeting held on 12 June 2002.

Your minute of this item should always end with a phrase such as:

The minutes were agreed as a correct record.

If the meeting agrees a correction to the minutes, this is recorded first. For example:

The meeting noted that on page 4, paragraph 3.1, 'Staff salaries will rise by 17 per cent' should read 'Staff salaries will rise by 1.7 per cent.' With this correction, the minutes were agreed as a correct record.

You should not retype and correct the set of minutes that are filed and archived. You may want to make a handwritten note drawing attention to the correction, but the official correction to the minutes is the one made by the group at the next meeting. If the archived set of previous minutes has been corrected, the subsequent minutes will not make sense.

Some groups like their minutes to be signed by the chair as a way of showing that the group has approved them. Others do not. You will need to find out what is the custom and practice for your group. If the chair does sign the minutes, make sure this happens straight away rather than allowing several months' worth of minutes to accumulate for signature. If the minutes are signed, the signature is usually either on the front sheet or on the last page. The signature should be dated or it will be invalid. Some meetings like the chair to initial each page – again, find out what the usual practice is for this group.

Numbering your minutes

This is a matter for individual organisations to dictate. Some organisations start each set of minutes at number 1. Others number their minutes through the calendar year – so a minute in January 2002 might be number 004/02. Some groups number their minutes consecutively throughout the life of the group. Some include initials to indicate the nature of the meeting – TB/02/001 – this would be the first minute in the year 2002 of a Trustee Board meeting.

Look at the last set of minutes to determine your numbering style and, if in doubt, as always, ask the chair. Be consistent both within each set of minutes and between different sets of minutes within the organisation. For example, if your first sub paragraph is numbered 1a then all subsequent sub paragraphs will use a letter style and so on. This is where it is useful to establish a house style that everyone will follow.

Matters Arising from the minutes

This item should deal only with quick items of a progress-chasing nature. It should not be an opportunity for the group to go over the whole of the previous meeting. This is something that should be established by the chair.

When recording Matters Arising, you will need to refer, in your minute heading, to the minute number in the previous minutes. Do not use the previous minute number as your sub paragraph number in these minutes as this can be confusing to the reader.

So, do put:

3   *Matters Arising*

3.1   *Staffing (Minute 4.2)*

3.2   *Conference (Minute 12)*

Don't put:

3   *Matters Arising*

4.2   *Staffing*

12   *Conference*

What to do if the chair moves an agenda item

It often happens that the order of the agenda is changed during the meeting, perhaps because some people have to go early or just because this now seems more logical.

When this happens, you must write the minutes in the order in which the meeting actually happened. So if agenda item 12 is discussed after agenda item 5, you minute it as minute number 6. It may be helpful to draw attention to the varying of the agenda in the text of the minutes:

> *The meeting decided that item 12 on the agenda would be discussed at this point.*

You may also want to refer to this in the minute heading. For example, if agenda item 12 is 'Conference', the minutes might read:

> *6   Conference (Agenda item 12)*

It is not good practice to minute the meeting as if it had happened in the order on the agenda if it did not. There are two reasons for this. One is that the minutes need to be a true record of the meeting. The discussion on each item will depend on what was discussed under previous items. For example, if the meeting decides, near the beginning of the meeting, that the organisation is bankrupt, this is likely to affect all subsequent discussions. It is not logical, and does not convey a true impression, if these discussions are recorded in a different order to that in which they took place.

Moreover, the agenda for a meeting does not have the official status of the minutes. The agenda is a guide for the meeting and the chair. The minutes are the official record and, in the case of many public bodies, have official legal status. The order of the meeting, as it really happened, is therefore more important than the order of the agenda.

Another problem is when an agenda item is referred to while another item is being discussed. For example, in the discussion on the finances, the conference budget is discussed although this is listed as a separate agenda item later. You should minute the discussion as it happened. Later, in the minute of the agenda item on the conference budget, you can refer to the earlier minute.

Example

12   Conference Budget

This item was discussed earlier in the meeting (see Minute 6).

Deferred items

If the meeting does not reach the end of the agenda and so does not discuss the last few agenda items, you should record this. For example:

Agenda items 20–26 were deferred until the next meeting.

If other action will be taken about the deferred items, such as referring them to the chair for 'chair's action', the minutes should make this clear.

Agenda items 20–26 were deferred until the next meeting excepting item 24, Christmas Party, which was referred to the Chair for Chair's Action.

Date of next meeting

At the end of the minutes, it is wise to record the date, time and venue for the next meeting, even if the group does not discuss this and it is not on the agenda. Many people are prompted to make a diary note by looking at the minutes when they come out and it is helpful to include this information here.

Time meeting closed

There is no need to record the time the meeting closed unless the standing orders or rules for the meeting specify that it should finish by a particular time. In these circumstances you need to record the closing time. If the meeting goes over the official closing time, there will have to be agreement by the meeting that this should happen. If there is no such rule for your meeting it is not necessary to record the closing time.

Below is the style guide from one of CSC's client organisations.

TITLE

DATE AND VENUE

(In Helvetica 12 (HELV12), Uppercase, bold and centred)

(Header and footer to appear on each page of documents with line)

All text to be in HELV12

Present: List names in alphabetical order, including title if appropriate, and highlight who is the Chair and Minute Taker.

1. WELCOME AND APOLOGIES (All main headings in uppercase and bold)

Start text here

2. MINUTES OF PREVIOUS MEETING (DATE)

Start text here

3. MATTERS ARISING (DATE)

Refer to previous meetings and list relevant items as follows –

3.1 Sub heading (all sub headings in sentence case and bold)

Start text here

3.2 Sub heading

Start text here

3.3 Sub heading

Start text here

4. OTHER MAIN HEADINGS

Start text here

Action: AB

(to be in bold and aligned right)

5. ANY OTHER BUSINESS

6. DATE OF NEXT MEETING

(agree venue, Chair and Minute Taker if appropriate)

8
Minutes style and grammar

Formal minutes are written in a different style to many other kinds of writing. They are much more likely to use the passive voice, which is nowadays considered very old fashioned in most forms of writing, and they tend to use longer sentences.

Passive voice

Use of the passive helps to emphasise the corporate nature of the minutes. To say 'It was decided' is less personal than to say 'We decided'. For this reason, minutes are far more likely to use the passive than any other form of writing such as letters or newsletters.

Thus, instead of writing '*The chair signed the minutes*', you would be far more likely to record '*The minutes were signed by the chair*'. In the same way, instead of writing '*The Chief Executive presented the paper*' you would probably record '*The paper was presented by the Chief Executive*'. Be careful with the phrase '*It was decided...*' This is used a lot in minutes. The correct form is '*It was decided **that**...*' This will then be followed by another passive form, for example 'It was decided that the conference would be held in Brighton'. It is not correct to write '*It was decided **to hold** the conference in Brighton*'.

The same rules apply to the phrases '*It was agreed...*' and '*It was noted...*' Both should be followed with the word '*that*'.

So:

> *It was agreed that the officers should staff the conference.*

> *It was noted that the fun day had been unsuccessful due to bad weather.*

Verbs

A frequent mistake in minutes is the use of incorrect verbs. This is because the minute taker **repeats** what the individual person said instead of **reporting** what the meeting did. When we describe a conversation or discussion that took place in the past, we move the tense of the verb back into the past form. For example, if someone said at the meeting:

'The treasurer *is* pleased with the new accounting systems.'

This would be minuted as:

*The meeting noted that the treasurer **was** pleased with the new accounting systems.*

In the same way, if the meeting heard:

'The organisation will be financially healthy next year.'

This would be minuted as:

*The meeting noted that the organisation **would** be financially healthy next year.*

The trick in doing this correctly is to mentally insert a phrase such as 'the meeting noted' or 'it was reported that'. You will not necessarily write these phrases at the beginning of each sentence or paragraph as this is unnecessarily cumbersome. However, if you remember that you are describing or recording what was said in the past rather than repeating the words used, you will have more chance of success.

Here are some examples:

At the meeting: '...the conference will be held in September.'

In the minutes: *It was noted that the conference would be held in September.*

At the meeting: '...the leaflet has gone out to all members.'

In the minutes: *The leaflet had gone out to all members.*

At the meeting: 'the Director is going to Africa immediately after the meeting.'

In the minutes: *It was noted that the Director was going to Africa immediately after the meeting.*

At the meeting: '... the organisers are responsible for minuting meetings.'

In the minutes: *It was agreed that the organisers were responsible for minuting meetings.*

At the meeting: '...all the events have been very successful.'

In the minutes: *...all the events had been very successful.*

Longer sentences

Minutes tend to use longer sentences than other forms of writing. This helps the minute taker summarise the discussion in a few phrases. An example of this would be a discussion where points raised included:

- A decision to hold a conference in Birmingham
- The conference venue in Birmingham is cheaper than the one in London
- The venue is easy to get to by public transport
- The refreshments are of high quality and reflect a variety of cultures
- The venue has good disability access

The minute for this discussion might read:

It was decided that the conference would be held in Birmingham as the venue was cheaper than the London venue; there was good access by public transport and good disability access; and the refreshments were of high quality and reflected a range of cultures.

This kind of longer sentence with several subordinate clauses is very frequently used in formal minutes. Do note that this kind of formality is unnecessary and inappropriate in informal notes.

Longer sentences help the minute taker wrap up several relevant discussion points at the same time. It is not necessary for these points to be recorded in the minutes in the order in which they are discussed at the meeting. The minute taker will gather points together logically to show how decisions were made (see Chapter 2).

Referring to background papers

Agenda items are often accompanied by background papers, sometimes very lengthy ones. The minutes need to refer to these and to note any passages which the meeting wants to highlight. For example:

The meeting noted the reference to care leavers in Chapter 4 of the document and felt that the recommendations did not go far enough.

Sometimes the meeting will use the recommendations set out in a background paper as the basis for its decision. By and large, the minutes should stand by themselves. It should not be necessary for a reader to know the whole content of a background paper in order to understand the minutes. However, having said this, it is not always best practice to rewrite all the recommendations into the minutes. It may be enough to record:

The meeting agreed the recommendations set out in the report.

When the minutes refer to a background paper, this should be filed and archived with the approved minutes and treated as part of the minutes themselves.

Useful terms for minutes

- **Proposed**

  Used when an idea or suggestion that has been put forward but is not yet agreed or decided, e.g. *It was proposed that the conference should be held in Birmingham.*

- **Resolved**

  Used where a proposal is decided by a formal process such as a vote, e.g. *The proposal was put to the vote and it was resolved that the conference should be held in Birmingham.*

- **Decided/agreed**

  Used where the group has taken a decision by consensus, e.g. *After discussion, it was agreed that the conference should be held in Birmingham.*

  NB The terms 'resolved', 'decided', and 'agreed' are often used in place of each other. We have given definitions and uses that are often used in minutes, but, as in many situations, there is no one right answer!

- Noted

  Used where a proposal, idea, situation or paper is received by the meeting but no decision is taken, e.g. *The meeting noted the government's forthcoming conference in Birmingham.*

- Referred

  Used where an item is sent to another body for decision. This could be 'higher up' the organisation such as a sub-committee referring an item to the board or it could be 'lower down' the organisation such as a board referring a matter to a sub-committee.

- Deferred

  Used where a decision on an item is postponed, for instance to a later meeting, e.g. *The decision on the conference venue was deferred to the next meeting.*

9
What to put in and what to leave out

We established in Chapter 2 that the main purpose of minutes is to record the decisions made by the group. Decisions are the framework around which the minutes should be written. They form the essential bones of the minutes and everything else should be written around them. So, your first criterion when deciding what to include is: **what was the decision?**

Decisions

There is always a decision on each agenda item. The decision may be to take a particular form of action – in which case an action point may be necessary. It may be to agree a policy or procedure. It may be to receive a document without discussing it further. It may be to note information and facts brought to the attention of the meeting. It may be to defer a decision until a later date, either because further information is needed or because the meeting cannot agree. Even a rambling discussion which seems to go nowhere is taking a decision: the decision to make no decision!

Always ensure that you understand what the group wants to do at the end of each agenda item. If necessary, ask the group or the chair. We discussed this in more detail in Chapters 4 and 5.

Other factors you need to consider will include the following:

- The main point
- Significance
- Relevance
- Controversial matters
- Need to know

The main point

Always try to summarise in your minutes. Do not include the exact wording of contributions but instead summarise the main point made by a participant. Better still, summarise several speakers' points together, if these form part of the same argument.

For example, if Fred says that the conference should be held in Birmingham because the venue there is on a main road with good parking facilities and Jane agrees and says that she has always liked Birmingham and found it easy to get to and Shauna contributes that there are good bus routes between the venue and the station in Birmingham, you do not need to minute this as three separate points. The **main point** of all three contributions is that the Birmingham venue is easy to get to both by car and by public transport.

Significance

Different items raised during the discussion will vary in their significance. For example, when discussing where to hold a conference, points raised might include the cost of the venues in different areas, access and travel arrangements, the quality of refreshments and the fact that someone's aunt lives there. While the other factors might be felt to be significant, the aunt is probably not! It requires understanding of the subject matter to be clear what is significant and what is not. This is why minute takers need to be able to understand the discussions they minute (see Chapter 3).

Relevance

Matters not relevant to the meeting, or not relevant to this discussion, should not be included in the minutes. For example if, in a discussion on where to hold a conference, the meeting notes that one venue will require more staff overtime to be worked than an alternative venue, this would be a relevant point. However, if the meeting then went on to discuss overtime at length the subsequent discussion would not be relevant to the venue for the conference and should be omitted.

Beware of meeting delegates who feel that their every word is relevant and should be minuted. This is not good practice. The minute taker should raise this with the chair for guidance.

Controversial matters

Where the subject under discussion is controversial or sensitive, you should include more detail in the minutes. For example, in a discussion on the conference venue, where a clear objective decision is taken to hold the conference in Birmingham and none of the delegates feel strongly about this a simple minute will be fine.

It was decided that the conference would be held in Birmingham.

However, if there are strong feelings and heated discussion, it may be better to include some of the main points of the discussion as well as the decision.

Having carefully considered the London venue, which offered greater facilities and better quality refreshments, it was decided that the conference should nevertheless be held in Birmingham as this venue was cheaper with better disability access.

The subject matter may be controversial at the meeting, as in the example above, or it may be of a generally sensitive nature. For example, if a group of doctors were discussing the use of a particular treatment that was known to have some adverse side effects, they would want to carefully record their reasons for recommending its use and the circumstances in which the treatment would be recommended. This kind of care would be necessary, even where the doctors themselves were all in agreement.

Need to know

When deciding what to include, always be aware of the audiences for the minutes. Who will read them and what do these people need to know? For example, when recording a discussion on the venue for a conference, possible audiences might be:

- Members of the organisation – they will want to know that their needs have been considered and their money well spent
- Trustees of the organisation – they will want to know that decisions were made on sound business grounds and that financial considerations were taken into account
- Staff of the organisation – they will need to know what they need to do next in order to organise the conference in the chosen venue
- Regulators, e.g. the Audit Commission, the Charity Commission or the Housing Corporation – they will want to know that the decision was taken on sound business grounds and in line with the rules for local authorities, charities or housing associations

10
Different kinds of meetings

Minuting information sharing sessions

It can be difficult for the minute taker if the group decides that each participant will do a briefing or presentation on the work in their area. This is a common practice in team meetings and the minute taker can never be sure how much detail is required in the minute for this item.

Here are some tips to help you with this.

Get everyone to provide you with a written brief

If you know, from the agenda or from previous meetings, that this kind of session is going to happen, you can let each participant know before the meeting that you will be asking for a few bullet point notes at the end. This will ensure that your minute covers the points they wanted to include. If the presentations are quite long, they have probably made notes anyway and a copy of these will be all that is necessary.

Stick to concise points if possible

On the whole, it is best to summarise such sessions as concisely as possible. People tend to go into detail when describing their own work. Ask yourself how much of this is necessary when writing up your minutes.

Consider what people reading the minutes will need to know

Remember – one of the golden rules of minutes is to write for your audience. If the people who read the minutes need lots of detail, then that is what you give them. They may need only a brief summary, perhaps with a note to speak to the relevant participants for further information. Or it may be entirely appropriate simply to minute:

Everyone shared information on what was happening in their team.

Get people to check their own information points

When minuting an information session, it is easiest to get each participant to check their own bullet points or paragraph. A quick email round the group asking for support on this and giving a deadline will save a lot of corrections at the next meeting.

Minuting presentations

When minuting presentations, a lot of the tips above apply. Think what your audience will need to know when they read the minutes. For example, if a team meeting hears a presentation from someone in Personnel about the new maternity leave arrangements, it may be enough to minute:

The group heard a presentation from Calvio Telesi from Personnel on the new maternity leave arrangements. Further information is available from Calvio or anyone in the personnel section.

However, if the personnel section are having a presentation from their manager on the new maternity leave arrangements, as part of a training and information session so that they can answer questions from colleagues, they will need a much more detailed minute to refer to later.

If possible, get the person giving the presentation to give you a copy of their notes. If they are using PowerPoint, this is simply a question of printing off the slides in a different format and very easy to do. However the presentation is given, the presenter will almost certainly have made notes of some kind and these will be useful if you feel you have to write the presentation up in detail.

When you have written the minute of the presentation, get the presenter to check it. This applies both to the account of the presentation itself and to any questions and answers that follow it. If you are recording these, then it is important to keep the answers accurate and the presenter is in the best position to do this.

Minuting case reviews

In social services and housing organisations, many minute takers have to record case reviews: meetings where the individual circumstances of each client are considered and action plans agreed. In such meetings, detail is important and the usual rules of concise summarising do not apply. Each speaker is probably an expert in their own field – the social worker, the housing officer, the health visitor, the physiotherapist. It is therefore likely that each person's contribution will have to be recorded in summary form and you will be much more likely than usual to refer to each speaker by name or by role.

Example

> *Ms Jones, Social Worker, was aware that the children were often asked to go shopping on their own and felt that this was inappropriate given their ages. Mr Smith, Health Visitor, agreed and said that the children had become the carers for the parent and that their health was suffering as a result. Ms Green, Physiotherapist, told the group that the client's health was unlikely to improve dramatically in the near future so the children's needs would have to be considered in the short and medium term.*

This is far more detailed than the usual business meeting minute but the detail is important in recording the progress of clients and the reasons for decisions and action plans made.

Minuting disciplinary or grievance hearings

These are also very different from the usual business meeting. Lay minute takers should not take minutes of these quasi-legal meetings unless they have support from their personnel or human resources department. The minutes of such meetings will be a much fuller record than those of a straightforward business meeting. They may be used later in an Employment Tribunal to show that the case was conducted fairly and according to best practice and employment legislation. Minute takers should take great care with these minutes, should not undertake them without advice and should insist on their being checked by a person qualified to do so.

11
Democracy

Many minute takers will be called on to minute meetings that involve the formal process of voting, proposals, amendments and so on. There are many rules and conventions that apply to such meetings and we do not aim to cover all of these here. The governing document for the meeting (Memorandum and Articles, constitution, terms of reference etc.) will specify the main rules for conducting the meeting and you, as the minute taker, must be familiar with these documents.

In a company registered with Companies House, there will be an appointed company secretary. It is this person's job to make sure that meetings are conducted in accordance both with the governing documents and with company law. If you are the company secretary, you would be wise to undertake specific training in this role. If you are not, do seek the advice of the company secretary when taking the minutes.

In this chapter we cover only the main rules for minuting formal voting procedures and some of the terms associated with this kind of meeting.

Annual General Meetings

One of the most common types of meetings to use voting procedures is the Annual General Meeting (AGM). Whether of a company or a charity, or in many cases both, AGMs have very specific rules for how votes are taken, how proposals can be received and amended, how nominations can be made and so on. These will be set out in the governing document and any accompanying by-laws or standing orders and you need to be aware of these if you are responsible for minuting an AGM.

Resolutions/proposals/motions

These are the policies/ideas/suggestions put to the meeting for approval. The terms 'resolution', 'proposal' and 'motion' are all more or less interchangeable in this context. In this book, we refer to proposals but there is no single correct term.

Proposals may have to be submitted in advance or they may be moved at the meeting itself. The proposal must have a 'mover' – i.e. someone who proposes it and will open the debate in favour of the proposal.

There must also be a 'seconder' – that is another person who is also prepared to put their name forward as being in favour of the proposal. This person has the right to speak in the debate but need not do so. If a proposal is moved and no one will second it, the proposal is said to 'fall' – i.e. it cannot be discussed. The logic behind this is that if only one person in the meeting feels the proposal is worth debating, there is no point in wasting the meeting's time on it.

The minute taker should ensure that the text of the proposal and the full name of the mover and seconder are available to those running the meeting. If the text has not been circulated in advance of the meeting, the chair should read it out before the vote is taken. The minute taker must record the text of the proposal and the name of the mover and seconder in the minutes. If those attending the meeting are there as representatives of branches or member organ-isations (e.g. in a national organisation with local branches) then the minute taker must record the name of the organisation or branch that the mover and seconder represent.

Example

Proposal:

That this AGM condemns the government's inaction on child poverty.

Moved: Asif Singh, East London Branch

Seconded: Jane Shaw, Nottingham Branch

Amendments

An amendment is an attempt to alter the wording of a proposal. The wording should show exactly how the text of the original proposal will be altered. Like a proposal, the amendment should have a mover and a seconder. If there is no seconder, the amendment will 'fall' and will not be discussed.

Example

Amendment:

After 'AGM', delete 'condemns' and add 'regrets'.

Moved: Shauna King, South Devon Branch

Seconded: Michael Kelly, West Midlands Branch

As minute taker, you must get the text of the amendment if this has not been previously circulated and the name (and where necessary the branch or organisation) of the mover and seconder.

Once an amendment has been moved and seconded, the debate should concentrate on the amendment rather than on the original proposal.

If an amendment is put to the vote and accepted by the meeting, it becomes part of the proposal. This is then sometimes referred to as the 'substantive' proposal – that is a proposal that has been success-fully amended – as opposed to the 'original' proposal – the one that was first put to the meeting.

Nominations

Governing documents will specify who may make nominations and who may be nominated. Like proposals, nominations must have a mover and a seconder. If these are taken at the meeting, it is the role of the minute taker to ensure that all these names are taken correctly so that the chair can put them to the meeting when the time comes to vote.

Voting

The chair will put the amendment, proposal or nomination to the vote and must take votes in favour, against and abstentions. There may be people appointed to assist the chair in counting the votes and these are sometimes called 'tellers'. They may be, but do not have to be, people who are independent of the organisation and do not have votes themselves. This is often seen as a way of ensuring the impartial conduct of the voting process.

If the meeting is a large one and there is a very clear majority, either in favour of the proposal or against it, the chair may decide not to count the votes. In this case, the minutes would read something like:

> *The proposal was accepted (or approved) by the meeting by a large majority of those voting.*

If the meeting does not accept this decision by the chair, they can ask for votes to be counted.

Where everyone entitled to vote votes in the same direction, either in favour or against, the vote is said to be 'unanimous'. Where there is a majority in favour or against and no votes in the other direction but there are some abstentions, the vote is said to be passed 'nem con'.

Example

In favour: *20 votes*

Against: *0 votes*

Abstentions: *0 votes*

The proposal was passed unanimously.

But:

In favour: *15 votes*

Against: *0 votes*

Abstentions: *5 votes*

The proposal was passed nem con.

The term 'nem con' is short for the Latin phrase '*nemine contradicente*' which means 'no one contradicting'. Clearly a 'nem con' agreement to do something would be weaker than a unanimous decision as it would imply that at least some people had abstained.

12
Effective listening

Listening effectively is something many minute takers worry about. No matter how conscientious you are, it can be very easy to allow your concentration to drift. Meetings are not always a matter of fascination to the minute taker and it is always harder to concentrate on subject matter that we don't find personally interesting.

There is also something unnatural about the task of the minute taker. In an ordinary conversation, we use tone of voice and body language to help us understand meaning. These tend to be much less helpful at formal meetings where minute takers are obliged to concentrate on the words alone. Below, we give you a few tips to improve your listening skills.

Look at the speaker

It is much easier to hear and understand someone we can see than someone who is hidden from us. Many people comment that they are less likely to understand the detail of a conversation on the telephone than one face to face. At the meeting, you need to be in a position to see everyone present. You also need to be able to look up while recording your notes so as to make eye contact with the speaker. This ability to look at someone while they are speaking will make it much easier for you to make sense of what they are saying.

Some people find it difficult to take notes without looking at the page. In these circumstances, you can either practise the skill until it becomes easier or you can take quick glances at the page while concentrating on the speaker. The ability to do this is a physical skill like swimming or riding a bicycle. It comes with practice and will become second nature when you have been doing it for a while.

Follow the flow of the discussion

It is unnecessary and unhelpful to record every word spoken during the debate. Your job is to understand the flow of the discussion and to get a feel of the main thrust of each speaker's contribution. Many minute takers panic because they miss a few words when listening. This panic then prevents them from hearing or understanding what comes next. If you understand the context well, you will be able to pick up the salient points without necessarily having heard or understood every word.

Get the content and the main points

Remember that when you listen, you are concentrating on under-standing the **main point**. Some people have a habit of mentally repeating in their head the words they write on the page. This is very dangerous when minute taking as you will drown out the speaker with your own silent repetition! Concentrate throughout the meeting on the main point you feel the speaker is making and how it will contribute to a decision.

It is also dangerous to get carried away with your own opinions about the subject under discussion. While you may have strong views, these are irrelevant to the meeting and it will not help you to record the meeting impartially if you are concentrating on your own views.

Make sure you note decisions

Remember that the decisions are the framework around which the minutes will be written. As you listen, constantly check out what kind of decision you think will be made on the basis of each speaker's contribution.

Keep focused on the discussion by taking notes

During the discussion, you may feel that the meeting has strayed off the agenda or that participants are not contributing relevant information. It is dangerous, at this point, to put your pen down and stop taking notes. If you allow your own thoughts to wander, you may find that the discussion has moved on and that you have missed relevant material. Keep jotting down the **main points** made by each speaker. You may find at the end of the discussion that they were relevant after all. Even if this is not the case, you will continue to be mentally alert to the meeting and will not be in danger of missing important points through inattention.

Remember that, although your notes are brief, they will probably contain far more material than you will use when you write up the formal minute. This is something we will come back to in Chapter 13.

Don't miss the next discussion because you're making notes on the last one

You must keep up with the meeting. Again, this is something that comes with practice. Brief notes, focusing only on key points will help, but the important thing is to keep up so that you are recording the meeting as it happens rather than what was said five minutes ago.

If you find this difficult, here is a simple exercise to help you. Make a video of a short section of a television programme. A discussion programme such as the BBC's *Question Time* is ideal for this. Tape about ten minutes' discussion then play the tape and listen while you take notes. At the end, rewind and play the tape back, looking at your notes. How accurate a record did you make? Did you keep up? Did you record the main points made by each speaker? Repeat this exercise every week for several weeks and you will find it becomes increasingly easy.

'Difficult' voices

Some people are harder to hear than others. Some people naturally speak softly. Others mumble or swallow their words. Some speak with a different accent to the ones you are used to. In all these circumstances, you need to focus your listening using all the tips listed above. Concentrate on trying to hear the main point and look at the speaker to help your understanding. If necessary, you can politely ask the speaker to speak up or slow down. With quiet speakers, a hand placed behind your ear is a good way of showing you can't hear them without saying so. If all else fails, you must ask them to repeat what they said. Failure to do this may result in discrimination against these speakers as their contribution will not find its way into the minutes!

Using a tape recorder

Some minute takers like to take a tape recording of the meeting, feeling that this will act as a back up if they miss anything. If you decide to do this, it is important to make sure that everyone at the meeting knows it is being recorded and has the opportunity to consent to this. Failure to do this may breach people's privacy rights.

A tape recording may help you remember difficult parts of the meeting. However, tapes can be unhelpful as well. Unless you have an expensive, high quality machine, it is unlikely that every contribution will be clear on the tape. Voices which are difficult to hear face to face will be even harder to distinguish on tape. And just when it really matters, the tape will come to an end and need turning over.

If you use a tape recorder, do use this as back up only – don't think it will substitute for your own carefully taken notes.

Personal comfort

A long meeting can be physically uncomfortable. Make sure that you use the loo before you start, that you don't drink too much coffee before or during the meeting, and that you are sitting in a reasonably comfortable chair with something firm to write on. Encourage the meeting, through the chair, to take comfort breaks at least every two hours. Use these breaks to walk briskly to the loo, perhaps go outside and get a few breaths of air, and generally invigorate yourself before you go back into the meeting. Finally, try to prevent the room becoming too hot. There is nothing worse for concentration than a hot, airless room!

If in doubt, ask!

If the meeting gets right away from you, you can ask the chair to summarise at the end to try to pick up any salient points you have missed. If this is not possible, try to find a colleague who was at the meeting to help you out. Don't bluff your way through in these circumstances as this could have serious consequences.

13
Taking effective notes

Taking notes for minutes requires a combination of skills. You must be able to understand the discussion and the different contributions. You must be able to record those contributions in a few abbreviated key words, ensuring enough clarity to give you sufficient recall for writing up the minutes later. And you must be able to come back to your notes later and make sense of them. No wonder many minute takers find note taking one of the hardest parts of the process.

Below we consider a few tips which can make note taking easier and more effective.

Use shorthand if you can

Shorthand is a great talent and very useful for minutes. However, it is not a requirement for minutes and many people take excellent notes without it. Shorthand is a formalised way of using symbols to express words so that you can write them down as fast as they are spoken. Shorthand users are taught to reproduce verbatim the words they hear – that is what shorthand is for.

This is not altogether helpful for minutes. We have already noted that minutes do not consist of a verbatim record. Shorthand users will need to distinguish, within their notes, what are the main points and what are the significant and relevant contributions. They therefore have to do, after the meeting, the job that non-shorthand users are beginning to do during the meeting – that is, deciding what to put in and what to leave out. Many shorthand users admit to minutes which are far too long. They have taken down the verbatim record and have failed to use it to record a concise summary of the arguments.

In conclusion, do use shorthand if you can, but use it to record only the key words and main points so as to have an accurate but concise record to use when writing up the minutes.

Use abbreviations of key words – make them consistent and understandable

The real art of note taking is to abbreviate. Writing only the key words in a contribution and abbreviating each word will enable you to keep up and to summarise more concisely later on.

Example

The speaker says, 'The conference should be held in Birmingham because the venue there is better. It is cheaper and has better disability access.'

Your notes for this contribution might look like this:

Conf = Birm cos ven better. Chper + better dis access.

One way of thinking about this is to look at the way we use text messages. This is a good example of using key words only and abbreviating them to write faster. Last December, my daughter sent me the following message:

WHT U WNT XMS?

I texted back:

PFM PLS

Sure enough, under the Christmas tree that year was a beautiful bottle of my favourite scent!

Another trick is to use symbols for common expressions. Thus, when I worked for the National Council of Voluntary Child Care Organisations, I used a capital N to stand for the very long name of the organisation! We can use arrows for increasing, improving, getting better: ↑. Or for decreasing, getting worse: ↓. Most people have an ampersand sign for the word 'and' or we can use the plus sign. A triangle of dots ∴ means therefore. The same triangle upside down ∵ means because. However, I usually just write 'cos' which I find just as quick.

You need to experiment with your own abbreviations and symbols. What we are aiming for is a personal version of shorthand, which allows us to record quickly and keep up, with a good level of recall.

There is really no substitute for practice in learning this skill and for those who find it difficult, I would commend the exercise in Chapter 12, p. 67.

Be sure to make your abbreviations clear and unambiguous. 'Diff' may mean either difficult or different and it will not always be clear from the context which one you mean. You can write 'diffc' for difficult and this will make the meaning clear.

Get the main points and leave out all the ifs and buts

Remember that your notes are a reminder of main points only. Avoid too much detail and keep to the key words in a contribution. You are not required to use the exact words used by the speakers in discussion, so if you can think of a quick way of summarising what someone has said, do use it.

Example

A speaker says in discussion, 'We should definitely book an additional number of speakers for the conference. We need a plethora of views to inform us of the many facets of opinion in this area of debate and we need to reflect this in the number of speakers on the platform.'

The notes for this contribution might look like this:

More spkers needed – lots pts of view.

Use headings and agenda numbers to guide you through

As you take your notes, do write clearly the number and heading of each agenda item as you go along. If you do not do this, and your notes are quite brief, there is a danger you will not be able to tell where one discussion item ended and the next began. If the order of the agenda is changed, make a clear note of this at the time (see Chapter 7).

Ask for spellings and explanations of difficult terms – perhaps after the meeting

Don't become obsessed with the spelling of an unfamiliar word so that you lose concentration on the main point of the discussion. Make the best attempt you can to spell the word phonetically and ask someone at the end of the meeting both to spell it for you and, if necessary, explain the meaning. If speakers use unfamiliar initials or acronyms, again you may want to ask at the end of the meeting for someone to explain these. On the other hand, if you feel that some of the meeting participants are also having difficulty understanding these terms, then it is better practice to ask for an explanation during the meeting.

Go through your notes at the end of the meeting

At the end of the meeting, take a few minutes to read through the notes you have made with a highlighter pen in your hand. This is the point at which your recollection of the meeting will be at its clearest. Make sure your notes make sense and that you can read them. Rewrite any really messy words that may not be comprehensible later on. Then, in each agenda item, underline or highlight what you now understand to be the main points made during the discussion. If you do this now, your minutes will write themselves when you sit down at the computer some time during the next 48 hours.

Taking notes with a laptop

The practice of taking a laptop computer to the meeting is now creeping in to some organisations. Some minute takers welcome this as they find it easier to type than to write with a pen. Others dread it as a barrier to concentration. Our advice would be to do what you find easiest. If a laptop helps and you have one available, by all means use it. However, do be aware of the issue of noise. Your laptop should have a quiet keyboard or it may be distracting to the meeting.

When using your laptop, do not try to write the final minutes as you go along. You are still using key words only and making brief notes. However, it may be easier to write them up on screen when your notes are right there in front of you. Another danger with a laptop is to include too much and write the minutes in the order the discussion took place instead of summarising and grouping items logically together. Remember your laptop is just an electronic notebook. The work of summarising the discussion should be just as carefully undertaken as if you had written your notes by hand.

Using your notes to write your draft minutes

Your notes will be a pretty full record of everything said at the meeting. They will be in the order of the contributions made by participants. In order to summarise concisely and group points logically together, you may want to go through your notes and group the ideas as you will write them up.

One way of doing this is simply to make a list of the main points made in the notes under each item. You have highlighted these before you left the meeting so this is not difficult to do. Then review your list and group the items together before you write up your minute.

Example

Conference discussion – list of main points

- *Venue London or Birmingham – Birmingham decided*
- *London good for shops and good venue*
- *Birmingham better for members out of London and cheaper*
- *Transport arrangements London*
- *Transport arrangements Birmingham*
- *Need for refreshments to reflect cultural diversity*
- *Importance of disability access*
- *Need for a good speaker – government minister?*

A logical grouping might be:

1   *Two venues considered.*

Points in favour of Birmingham

- *better for members outside London*
- *cheaper*
- *good transport arrangements*

Points in favour of London

- *good venue*
- *shops*

Decision Birmingham – action point Jane Smith

2   *Equal opportunity considerations*

- *Importance of disability access*
- *Refreshments to reflect cultural diversity*

3   *Other points*

- *Need for good speaker – government minister – action point chief executive*

Another way of doing this is to use mind-mapping techniques.

Example

For the same discussion: see figure opposite

Some examples of notes at meetings

Example 1

Discussion

- 'The organisation should close down over Christmas, we never get any calls then and we could save money on heat and light bills.'
- 'There could be a crisis and people might need us.'
- 'Could we have a skeleton staff – perhaps one field officer and one press officer?'
- 'They could work from home and liaise by mobile phone.'
- 'Will staff have to be paid if we close down or will they take leave?'
- 'My department won't like taking their annual leave then – they might want to save it for the summer.'

Mind-mapping the conference discussion

Use the circles to highlight your main topics within the minute and link ideas together with the arrows.
Use the diagram to help you structure your minute as you write it up.

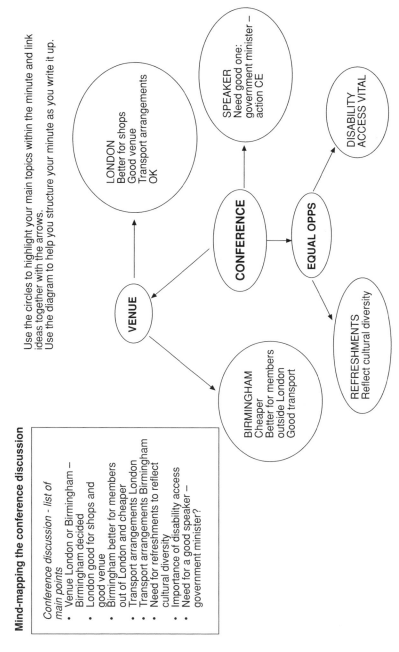

Conference discussion - list of main points

- Venue London or Birmingham – Birmingham decided
- London good for shops and good venue
- Birmingham better for members out of London and cheaper
- Transport arrangements London
- Transport arrangements Birmingham
- Need for refreshments to reflect cultural diversity
- Importance of disability access
- Need for a good speaker – government minister?

VENUE

CONFERENCE

EQUAL OPPS

LONDON
Better for shops
Good venue
Transport arrangements
OK

SPEAKER
Need good one:
government minister –
action CE

DISABILITY
ACCESS VITAL

REFRESHMENTS
Reflect cultural diversity

BIRMINGHAM
Cheaper
Better for members
outside London
Good transport

Notes

AJ   *Close down xmas – no calls – save money heat, light*

RB   *Crisis? Staff need us?*

JH   *skel staff? 1 fld off + 1 press off*

MY   *Wk home w mobiles*

RB   *Pay? Or A/L?*

SL   *Dept won't like A/L – save for summer*

Minute

The meeting considered a proposal that the organisation close over the Christmas period in order to save money on heat and light. Any potential crises could be dealt with by having two staff on duty – a field officer and a press officer who would work from home using their mobile phones. In considering whether staff would be required to take annual leave in the event of a closure, it was noted that this would not be universally popular.

Example 2

Discussion

- 'Where are we going to hold this year's conference? Some people want it in Birmingham this year.'
- 'We have always had it in London before. People like to come up for the shopping.'
- 'The London venue is very good – good disability access and the refreshments are yummy.'
- 'Yes but I do feel the members outside London are getting restless. They feel we don't care about them.'
- 'If we have it in Birmingham, we'll just have trouble from other parts of the country.'
- 'All right, let's have it London this year but announce we'll definitely have it somewhere else next year. Agreed?'
- 'Yes, agreed.'

Notes

AB   *Conf venue – Birm?*

CU   *Always London – ppl like shops*

PV   *London good – dis access + food gd*

AB   *Membs ex Lond not happy – we don't care*

CV   *If Birm trble other plces*

AB   *Lon this yr – annce swhere else nxt yr – agreed*

Minute

*The meeting considered the venue for this year's Annual Conference and **agreed** on a London venue for this year. Although Birmingham had been raised as a possible venue which would be popular with West Midlands members, other regions might feel differently and the London venue had provided a good service in the past besides offering access to shops and other facilities. However, since there was feeling from outside London that the venue should be moved, it was **decided** that a new venue would be sought for the following year.*

Example 3

Discussion

- 'We ought to try to introduce a flexitime scheme. Lots of other organisations have one and we ought to be more family friendly.'
- 'Wouldn't it be a nightmare trying to staff the office – we'd never know who was supposed to be in?'
- 'I think flexitime would be great – lots of our staff have children and it would help us retain them within the organisation.'
- 'It would need to be carefully thought through – we'd need something like core hours when everyone was supposed to be at work – say between 10.00 and 4.00.'
- 'We should work something up and consult with staff if we're going ahead.'
- 'Agreed. Let's get a draft consultation paper to our next meeting. Graham, will you write that?'
- 'OK.'

Notes

GH   *flexitime schm – other orgs have – more fam frndly*

BY   *nightmare! – who's in when?*

TY   *Flex = gd – lots staff have chn – help retain*

JH   *careful tht thru – core time? – 10–4*

GH   *wk up paper + consult stff*

TY   *Agd. GH to write draft cons ppr.*

Minute

*The meeting considered a proposal that the organisation introduce a flexitime scheme. While there was some concern that it might be difficult to know which staff were working, it was also noted that flexitime would help retain staff with children and that it would be possible to ensure that everyone was working during core hours e.g. 10.00 am to 4.00 pm. It was **agreed** that Graham Harwood, Assistant Director, would write a draft consultation paper which will come to the next meeting for discussion.*

Action: GH

14
Some checklists
for minute takers

Before the meeting

- ❏ Have I read the minutes of the last meeting?
- ❏ What other reading do I need to do to prepare for the meeting?
- ❏ Do I understand the subject matter on the agenda?
- ❏ If not, where can I get help?
- ❏ Do I have enough copies of all the papers for the meeting including the minutes of the last meeting?
- ❏ If the chair signs the minutes, have I prepared a copy for signing?
- ❏ Are my papers in good order, in a ring-bound file with the agenda items clearly marked?
- ❏ Is the room set out as the participants want it?
- ❏ Do I know the chair of the meeting?
- ❏ If not, what can I do to enhance my professional relationship with the chair?
- ❏ Have I arranged to sit next to the chair? If not, where will I sit?
- ❏ Have I asked the chair for a few minutes' briefing on the agenda? When will this happen?
- ❏ Have I diarised time to write the minutes up after the meeting?
- ❏ Have I prepared an attendance list for circulation at the meeting?
- ❏ Do I have all the stationery I need for the meeting including paper and at least two pens?

During the meeting

- ❏ Have I circulated the attendance list and has everyone signed it?

- ❏ Do I have an accurate record of all those who have given their apologies?

- ❏ Am I using the chair's opening summary in each agenda item to alert me to the likely nature of the decision?

- ❏ Am I aware of the speakers in the discussion and am I helping the chair ensure that anyone who wants to speak can do so?

- ❏ Am I focusing on the key points made by each speaker and how these relate to the decisions to be made?

- ❏ Are my notes brief and abbreviated and do they relate to the decisions the group is making?

- ❏ Am I remembering to concentrate on the meeting and continuing to make notes throughout for this purpose?

- ❏ Am I clear about the decision on each agenda item and, if not, can I ask the chair to clarify?

- ❏ Have I noted all action points carefully with the name/initials of the person responsible and a deadline where appropriate?

- ❏ Have I made a note of the date, time and venue of the next meeting?

- ❏ Have I gone through my notes ensuring I can understand and read back all key words and highlighting the main points in each agenda item?

After the meeting

- ❏ Have I got the chair's signature on the minutes of the previous meeting (where necessary) and have I filed and archived these carefully as the approved record?

- ❏ Have I started to write up my first draft of the minutes within 48 hours of the meeting?

- ❏ Are the minutes formal or informal?

❏ What numbering and house style will be used? Is there a template for this?

❏ If the minutes are formal, am I remembering to use the passive voice and to use the correct verbs when recording discussion points?

❏ Am I summarising discussions in concise form, using longer sentences to wrap up several related discussion points?

❏ Have I read the minutes over before sending them to the chair for their approval?

❏ Have I given the chair a clear deadline for their approval of the draft minutes?

❏ Will the minutes go out as soon as the chair has approved them or with the papers for the next meeting?

❏ If the minutes are going out straight away, have I highlighted action points for individual recipients?

❏ If the minutes are going out with the papers for the next meeting, do I need to prepare a separate action sheet?

❏ When the minutes are filed, which of the background papers need to be filed with them?

" BELIEVE ME, GOOD MINUTES CAN SAVE HOURS"

Index

Compiled by Sue Carlton

About the author

Jan Burnell specialises in management and governance training and consultancy. She has worked in senior roles in the public and voluntary sectors and has been Chief Executive of two national charities. She has been a local government councillor and the chair of a housing association. In all these roles she has learned to really appreciate the value of good minutes and is passionately committed to ensuring that the demanding role of the minute taker is seen as a pivotal one in any meeting.